FUN WITH FIDGET SPINNERS

50 SUPER COOL TRICKS & ACTIVITIES

DAVID KING OF GeekBite

WITH COLLEEN DORSEY & KATIE WEEBER

DESIGN ORIGINALS

an Imprint of Fox Chapel Publishing
www.d-originals.com

Don't miss the awesome Spin Games throughout this book. They will take your fidget game to the *NEXT LEVEL!*

Fidget Spinning Tips!

We have placed all sorts of tips and tricks throughout this book to help you achieve that next level of fidgeting status. Keep an eye out for these black boxes and you should have no problem showing off your best tricks at the next fidget throwdown.

"STOP FIDGETING" AND OTHER BAD ADVICE

You've probably heard it from your parents or your teachers: "Stop fidgeting!" Or maybe: "Please sit still!" When you're doing something that requires concentration, like studying or listening in class, you're supposed to sit quietly, focus, and do your work from start to finish without interruption. If you find this way of working frustrating, you're not alone! Sitting still is hard for lots of people, not just you.

In fact, we're learning more and more that trying to sit still and focus is counterproductive, and that most people work best when they have something else to do. Scientists have found that when kids use fidget toys, attention and focus in the classroom setting seem to get better. In story after story, a hyperactive kid finds a new sense of calm and balance when there's a fidget spinner in his hand. But the jury is still out on exactly how helpful fidget spinners are. This is no surprise, really, since these gadgets are so new to our culture.

While there might not be a ton of research out there on fidget spinners specifically, there have been studies about the act of fidgeting itself. Scientists who study how adults behave at work have found that fidgeters live longer than non-fidgeters because even a little bit of motion is better than no motion. Another well-established discovery is that taking short "brain-breaks" actually increases attention. If your parents are supposed to move around at the office and take breathers from their work, why not you! After all, tests are hard and there's not much downtime at school.

But why is fidgeting so effective for some people in aiding concentration? One reason just might be how we're hardwired as a species. Think about it. Once upon a time, people spent most

The Origin Story

You probably won't believe it, but the fidget spinner has been around in different forms since 1993! Many credit Catherine Hettinger with the invention of this toy. At the time, Catherine was recovering from an illness that left her very weak. In order to play with her seven-year-old daughter, Catherine needed a toy that was lightweight and didn't take a lot of energy to operate, but also something that was fun and would hold her daughter's attention. Catherine used stuff lying around her house to rig up a little spinny thingy—the first fidget spinner. It was a hit with her daughter, so Catherine continued to refine her design and eventually patented it in 1997. Sadly, toy companies weren't ready for her invention, and Catherine unfortunately let her patent expire in 2005. Some say that if Catherine had held on to her patent, she'd be swimming in offers for her cool design today. Others argue that today's fidget spinners differ enough from Catherine's design that her patent wouldn't cover them. Check out the research online. What do you think?

What Is a "Fidget"?

Here are some examples of fidgets that adults commonly use, and they may work for you, too. Remember, a true fidget should not distract from your primary task, and it should not be distracting to others in your classroom. Some more active fidgets like walking or spinning in a chair can be done at home. Common fidgets: playing with your hair or clothes; doodling; walking; bouncing, spinning, or rocking your chair; listening to music without lyrics or other white noise; chewing gum; tapping or playing with your pen.

of their days hunting, farming, or foraging for food. Fidgeting would have been a waste of precious energy. While we don't live that way anymore, our bodies are still built for that lifestyle—always ready for action. No wonder we want to stay in motion! Fidgeting is how we modern humans let out some of that bottled up, leftover energy.

Another reason fidgeting is useful, especially when it comes to concentration, is that it can keep your mind from wandering and help you focus on the task at hand. By engaging in some minor physical activity, you occupy the part of your brain that's likely to get bored. This way, the rest of your brain is free to concentrate on your teacher, your homework, or your science project and is not distracted by questions like: When is class over? What am I going to have for lunch today? The fidgeting takes the place of that mind wandering.

Just because fidgeting is good for you doesn't mean you should start running laps around your classroom or playing games with your classmates while your teacher is talking. Believe it or not, a "fidget" has specific limits attached to it. The important thing, according to experts, is that it is felt and not watched. Easy to ignore, in other words. The fidget can't be something so interesting that it takes over your full concentration. So, no, you can't claim that playing video games will help you finish your homework, but pressing buttons on a disconnected controller might!

It's also important that your fidget is not distracting to others. It seems like every other day another school puts the kibosh on fidget spinners in the classroom. Entire districts from Chicago to Brooklyn have banned them. The reason many teachers don't like them is, they say, that even students who don't have their own fidget spinners are distracted by the showing off of those who do. The white noise that spinners make can also be irritating during quiet work sessions, like during a test. If you happen to be one of the lucky students who's still allowed a spinner at your desk, try to keep it that way by using your spinner as a tool for concentration when class is in session and saving the tricks for outside of school.

Whether you believe that fidget spinners help you cope with anxiousness or that they're cool toys and nothing more, it's a good idea to enjoy them without letting them distract you from what's really important (like your grades). You can use them to dazzle friends, classmates, and family with your feats of dexterity. They can be an exciting puzzle for you to figure out the physics of spinning objects. With no logging on or levels to beat, they let you do something with your hands that also relaxes your mind. Best of all, they can give you those little brain breaks that make everything else in your day feel more satisfying. Fidgeting is healthy! Keep that in mind the next time someone tells you to stop playing with your fidget spinner and concentrate. And then ask them what *their* favorite fidget toy is...

In this book, we show you all about spinners—how they work, what types are available, and how to get the most out of yours so that you'll be a spin master in no time. So let's get started, and, yes, keep up that spinning!

Remember:

Always fidget responsibly! Use your spinner in class for concentration and outside the classroom for fun.

CHAPTER 1:
Ready, Set, Spin:
ALL ABOUT SPINNERS

So you have a collection of fidget spinners and have had some fun with them. Now—how can you make them go faster and learn some epic tricks that will secure your fidget spinner mastery? To help boost your spinner speed and trick difficulty, it might help to learn a little bit about how your fidget spinner is made and how it works. Fidget spinners are not just toys—they're actually little machines with a whole lot of physics behind them. With the power of knowledge on your side, the next time a teacher or parent scoffs at you for spinning your "toy," you can school them with a physics lesson, fidget-spinner style.

HOW THEY'RE MADE

Your fidget spinner has four basic parts: a central spinning hub (usually a ball bearing), the housing, weights, and caps (or fingerpads).

Ball Bearing

If you've ever used a skateboard or ridden a bicycle, you've experienced ball bearings in action. They're the things that make other things go around. A ball bearing has four parts: outer ring, inner ring, balls, and the retainer holding the balls in place. The outer ring is attached to the spinning part of an object, while the inner ring is attached to the stationary part.

Why is this important? Ball bearings are perfect for fidget spinners because they help reduce friction. Friction is resistance against motion. Try this: rub your hands together and see how fast you can make them go. Friction is the thing that keeps your hands from going super-fast. Now try it again with a tennis ball between your hands—faster, right? When the rubbing, sliding motion is replaced with a rolling motion, your hands move faster and quieter because there's less friction—less resistance against the motion. The balls in a ball bearing do the same thing for your fidget spinner. Cool, right?

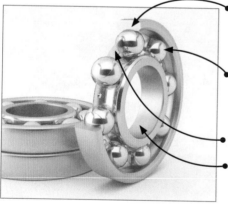

OUTER RING: I spin! I'm connected to the body of your fidget spinner and spin with it.

BALLS: I help your fidget spinner go faster and longer by reducing friction.

RETAINER: I hold the balls in place.

INNER RING: I don't spin. I'm connected to your fidget spinner's bearing caps, where your fingers go.

BEARING TYPES: There are only two kinds of ball bearings that work in fidget spinners: the 608 and the r188. Here's the breakdown:

608. ⅞″ (22mm) outer diameter, ⁵⁄₁₆″ (8mm) inner diameter, ⁹⁄₃₂″ (7mm) wide. The 608 is the bearing that skateboard wheels use. Large and sturdy, it's easy to install and clean, and very easy to find in stores.

r188. ½″ (13mm) outer diameter, ¼″ (6mm) inner diameter, ³⁄₁₆″ (5mm) wide. Most spinner experts are saying that the r188 is faster than the 608 because its smaller size allows for a bigger housing, which means more mass for spinning, and less mass at the non-spinning core. The r188 is the premium bearing choice for fidget spinners.

Bearings are traditionally made of steel, and you will find steel bearings are the most affordable and the most widely available. However, if you want to splurge for a proven upgrade, take advantage of a recent innovation in the ball bearing industry and look for ceramic ball bearings, made from silicon nitride.

CLOSURES: Very often, ball bearings have closures. Closures are flat rings placed above and/or below the outer ring, hiding the rolling balls from view and shielding the ball bearing from contaminants. The type of closure used for the ball bearing in your fidget spinner will impact its performance.

No closure. Offers the least protection, but also causes the least friction. Cleaning them is a cinch.

Metal closure. Offers some level of protection, and, since it doesn't make contact with the inner ring, causes very little friction. Easy to pry out and fit back in.

Rubber/Teflon™ closure. Offers the most protection but also the most friction. Difficult to remove and put back.

For fidget spinners, the best option is either to have no closure at all or a metal closure. Rubber or Teflon™ closures should be avoided because they make it harder to get the bearing spinning.

Housing

Housing is a fancy word for the main body of your fidget spinner. It holds, or "houses," the central ball bearing and the weights at the end of each arm. The housing is the fun, colorful part of your spinner that can be customized and transformed to match your personal taste and style. Housings are made of numerous materials. The most important thing for performance is that your spinner's housing is well balanced for fast, even spinning, but it's also important that it feels good in your hand and you like the way it looks!

WEIGHTS

HOUSING

WEIGHTS

WEIGHTS

SYNTHETIC: Plastic, rubber, silicon, carbon fiber composite. Factory-made spinners come in all sorts of exciting finishes. Weatherproof and indestructible, synthetic spinners will last long enough to be handed down to a little brother or sister once you've upgraded.

METAL: Aluminum, steel, brass, titanium. The benefits of metals are obvious—they feel cool and powerful in your hand, they shine and reflect light, and they have a satisfying sheen whenever they're in fast-spinning motion.

NATURAL: Ceramic, wood, paper, cardboard. Fidgeting and handling soothing, raw materials harvested sustainably is a satisfying combination. No factory needed: natural materials lend themselves to DIY or crafting projects if you have the tools and the time to learn.

FUNKY MONKEY: Dominoes, Legos®, paracord, metal nuts. These are the realm of the DIY spinnerhead. If you have the patience for YouTube how-tos, or maybe if you have some out-of-the-box creativity, you might be able to whip up a dazzling spinner out of something no one else would think of (check out the spinner made of Starburst® candy!).

Weights

The ball bearing provides a central hub around which your spinner spins, and the weights are what help it keep spinning. They add mass, which increases momentum. Try this: spin in a circle holding your arms close to your sides and see how long you can go. Are you tired yet? It takes a lot of energy on your part to spin this way. Now try it again with your arms out wide and straight across from each other—you can spin all day! This is because you've spread your weight out across a greater area.

It works the same way with your fidget spinner: in addition to the central hub (the ball bearing), there needs to be a way to spread out its weight to hold all its spinning energy. That's why your fidget spinner has arms.

Now here's where the weights come in. To increase the momentum of these spinning arms, add weight. Think of yourself spinning in place again. What happens if, in addition to holding your arms out wide, you were also holding a small dumbbell in each hand? You might spin so fast you lose control! It's the same with your fidget spinner. There are all sorts of weights that can be used to rev up your spinner.

ADDITIONAL BALL BEARINGS: Your typical, mass-produced fidget spinner uses other ball bearings to add weight to the arms, giving the spinner a totally symmetrical look. In this case, steel bearings are always better than ceramic—no need for premium spinning capability when the bearings aren't doing much spinning.

COINS: Coins make great spinner weights—they're heavy and perfectly round. Moreover, they come decorated, which is a plus if you happen to be a fan of Thomas Jefferson or Honest Abe! The trouble is that a single coin weighs much less than your typical ball bearing, which means you'll have to glue multiple coins together to get the same weight.

NUTS AND BOLTS: A trip to the hardware store can yield some heavy, hardcore weights for your fidget spinner. Some people even make entire spinners out of things like nuts, bolts, and washers. These are a great option for 3D-printed or DIY fidget spinners.

Venom Defense & Design, www.venomdd.com

FidgetHQ, fidgethq.com

Caps

Caps are the flat discs that cover the top and bottom of the central ball bearing on your fidget spinner so you can hold onto it more easily. Because it's where your fingers go, caps are sometimes called fingerpads. A great way to customize your fidget spinner is by embellishing with decorative bearing caps. Caps snap easily into the inner ring of ball bearings; usually all you need to get them in and out (for cleaning or replacement) is finger strength.

With caps you can color coordinate, personalize, and add bling with options like monograms, sports teams, superhero symbols, and more—the options are endless! In fact, shopping for caps can be almost as fun as shopping for spinners. You can find particularly snazzy caps that feature logos that include the Thundercats, the Cadillac logo, the American flag in blue, green, and gold—even the Sriracha logo!

First, though, get a feel for your own preferences. Since your fingers will be spending a lot of time holding onto your spinner's caps, it makes sense to get caps that feel just right. What material feels best to you? Molded plastic, copper, aluminum, maybe wood? What about shape? Some caps have a concave shape that allow your fingertips to dip in. Other caps have the opposite shape—convex—that means the caps stand out from the fidget spinner. Still other caps are perfectly flat.

If minimalism is your thing, you can express yourself without the logos, too. Fidget makers online are selling monochromatic plastic caps that come in dozens of colors. Meanwhile, other startups are offering custom-machined metal caps—grooved aluminum, solid brass, or even titanium—for big bucks. Remember, if you're going to customize your caps, the most important detail to keep in mind is the inner diameter of your ball bearing (see page 11).

CLEANING

Cleaning may not sound like a lot of fun, but it's the best way to maintain your spinner's speed and performance. In fact, almost every hack you'll find online to make your spinner go faster and longer has to do with cleaning and/or lubricating the bearing. So, think of cleaning your spinner less like a chore and more like tuning up a racecar.

If the bearing has caps (fingerpads), remove them to expose the bearing. If your bearing has a closure, carefully remove it by using a mini screwdriver. Place the spinner in a jar or can and add enough rubbing alcohol to cover it. If your spinner has removable bearings, you can just soak those rather than the entire spinner. Swirl the rubbing alcohol around a bit with a cotton swab or a plastic utensil to work it into the bearing, then let it soak for a few minutes. Swirl the rubbing alcohol again—you will see it getting dirty as it dissolves and breaks down the contaminants in the bearing.

While your spinner is soaking, clean the bearing closure and caps with warm, soapy water. Wipe them dry immediately. When you're finished soaking your spinner, dry it immediately using paper towels. If you've used anything other than rubbing alcohol, be sure to dry it with a hairdryer (set on cool!), as any leftover water can start to corrode the steel. For best performance, add a synthetic bearing lubricant designed specifically for small, fast-turning bearings. Skateboard lubricants work great. If you have ceramic bearings, cut the lubrication dose in half. Now it's time to reassemble your spinner and watch your spin speed increase by epic proportions!

RUBBING ALCOHOL

CHAPTER 2:
The Good, the Better, and the Totally Awesome:
TYPES OF SPINNERS

Half the fun of the fidget spinner craze is checking out all of the unique spinner designs and variations. Most fidget spinners are built around one of these basic shapes: figure eight, triangle, wheel, square, and hexagon. But that hasn't stopped legions of creative people from putting their own spin on these fundamental designs. So no matter what your personal style is, there's a totally awesome fidget spinner out there for you. Check out this guide to the different fidget spinners available, plus some other fidget toys that aren't spinners at all!

THE TRI

Everyone knows the most common type of fidget spinner! It's easy to use one handed and is designed for great spin times.

THE BI-WING

FidgetHQ, fidgethq.com

Beware—with its refined look, this design is a favorite for adults! But it might be a great fit for you, too. If you have small hands, you may find the bi-wing is easier to use than some of the other spinner designs.

THE HEX

Also called the "six post" or "six winged" fidget spinner, this design has become a bit of a classic. Often, each prong features evenly spaced rings of color that blur into stripes when spinning—and some are available with a glow-in-the dark band!

THE QUAD

With four prongs, this design forms an X or square shape. The weights forming the X can take on a number of shapes, from rounded prongs to sharp-looking claws—even a skull and crossbones!

Spinetic Spinners, www.spinetic-spinners.com

THE WHEEL

This design looks like it will keep spinning forever once it's set in motion. You can find loads of color variations to create cool effects as the wheel is spinning.

WeFidget, www.wefidget.com

THE MINI

Who wouldn't love a micro-sized fidget spinner? This design encompasses any spinner 2" in diameter or less. While the designs may be physically tiny, they are hugely popular!

THE FIDGET CUBE

Not only does this fidget toy spin, it also clicks, switches, dials, and glides. There's even a side of the cube that has a depression where your thumb can take a break and just rest. It's a lot of fun in a small package, and there's a twelve-sided version with even more fidgeting activities!

Jessica Huang, www.kieroncollective.com

THE FIDGET PAD

This fidget toy looks like a miniature video game controller. Like the fidget cube, it features buttons and dials for fidgeting, but it's large enough to keep both hands busy at the same time.

THE FIDGET FLIP

The latest fidget toy to surf in on the spinner wave is the "fidget flip," also called the "fidget roller." Instead of spinning, it topples end-over-end on a flat surface and always ends up vertical because of the way its weight is distributed.

Austin Hull, 2blackdogz.etsy.com

THE HALL OF FAME

There are hundreds, thousands, maybe millions of fidget spinner designs out there—they could fill whole books by themselves! Have fun exploring all of your options, and in the meantime, enjoy our favorites, which have made it into this hall of fame!

The Orbiter™, made from titanium and neodymium magnets.

The Nextri. A stainless steel body spins around a removable r188 bearing.

The REVOQ: a spinner with rolling and clicking steel balls, switches, and a mood stone. The central caps have grooved edges for idle turning.

The Apex. The slots on the wings—12 of them—can fit glass vials filled with glow material. The entire body is contoured.

WeFidget's Mini Original BAT spinner. It has a removable r188 bearing.

CHAPTER 3:
Spinner Tricks and Games

Now that you know why fidgeting is good for you and all about the different fidget spinners you can use, it's time to have some fun! You can do some pretty awesome stuff with your spinners beyond just fidgeting. Check out these totally awesome and epic tricks you can learn to show off your fidget spinner mastery. Be sure to keep an eye out for handy tips about increasing speed and spin time and some eye-catching modifications. Use the workbook in Chapter 4 to track your progress on your way to spin master glory.

THE ONE-FINGER BALANCING ACT

To kick off this wonderful book on fidget spinner tricks, we need to start with the basics. Don't worry, we'll step it up and get real crazy with the tricks later on, but we'll start off easy. To pull off The One-Finger Balancing Act, grip your spinner between the thumb and index finger of one hand. Then, give that sucker a firm spin. Slowly balance the spinner on your index finger, holding your finger straight up in the air like you're Michael Jordan balancing a spinning basketball. ***Challenge: Try tossing the spinner onto one of your other fingers, keeping it spinning as you do.***

SPIN GAME: Spinner Battles

Play this game with a partner. Sit across from each other with a table between you and a fidget spinner in front of each of you. Get your spinners going, then push them toward one another. As soon as the spinners touch, hands off! The last spinner spinning wins! *Hint: A spinner with extra weight at the end of its arms will do well in a spin battle!*

THE BASIC TOSS

To perform The Basic Toss, grip your spinner between the thumb and index finger of one hand and get it spinning. Then, toss the spinner to your other hand, catching it between your thumb and index finger. *Pro Tip: Keep eye contact with your friends as you perform the toss to show them who's the toss boss!*

Painting Plastic

Before you add any paint to your shiny, plastic fidget spinner, you'll need to do just a bit of prep work to ensure awesome results. Use some fine-grit sandpaper to scuff your fidget spinner, rubbing off some of the gloss so the paint will stick better. Wipe with a clean cloth and then grab your paintbrush!

THE HOT POTATO

Trick Level - **BEGINNER**

To do The Hot Potato, simply repeat The Basic Toss (page 25) over and over, tossing your spinner back and forth between each hand. You can even yell, "Hot! Hot! Hot! Hot! Hot!" if you want for added effect. ***Challenge: Try playing Hot Potato with a friend, tossing the spinner back and forth to each other.***

SPIN GAME: Hot Potato

The hot potato game is challenging to play and only for experienced fidgeters. Here's how to play. Get together with some of your friends in a circle. Spin the hot potato (your fidget spinner) and then softly throw it to someone in the circle, so they can catch it. Continue throwing the spinner around the circle until someone drops it. If you drop it, you're out! Keep going until you have one player left standing.

THE TOE SPINNER

The Toe Spinner is a lot like The One-Finger Balancing Act (page 24), but a bit less hygienic. As you have probably already deduced, the toe spinner entails spinning the fidget spinner on your toe. Staying perfectly still is the key to this trick. Start with your foot resting on the ground so you can stay steady. ***Challenge: Try standing on one foot, holding your other foot in the air and balancing the spinner on your toe. See how long you can hold that spin master pose!***

Metal Spinner Fix-up

Is your metal spinner not going as fast as it did right out of the box? There's a good chance that the bearing caps on the center bearing have become loose. Just screw the caps on tight and give the spinner a whirl. Back in action!

Columbia River Precision, www.crpspinners.com

THE NOSE SPINNER

To pull off The Nose Spinner, you'll need to focus hard on remaining very still. Start by tilting your head back and pointing your nose to the sky. Place the center of the spinner on the tip of your nose and hold it there with your index finger. Use your other hand to spin the spinner and see how long you can balance it on your nose. *CAUTION: Be careful with this trick; make sure you don't tilt your head back so far that you get a fidget spinner in the eye. While you're learning, you may want to wear a pair of sunglasses. They'll make you look super cool and provide protection at the same time.*

The Ultimate Upgrade

You can convert the coveted r188 bearing to a 608 bearing size to fit it in your spinner. All it takes is a little adapter called a "bearing core." Available from online specialty shops, these little metal rings fit snugly around any r188 ball bearing to pad it out to the size of a 608 bearing, which is able to fit into most commercial fidget spinners.

The Kong 3-in-1 is both a micro spinner and a bearing core.

FidgetHQ, fidgethq.com

THE FIDGET SANDWICH

For this delicious trick, you'll need to have two fidget spinners handy. Take one and stack it on top of the other. Hold the fidget sandwich between the thumb and index finger of one hand and get those bad boys spinning! Try spinning them in opposite directions for extra cool points. Remember, although they look delicious, fidget spinners are not for eating. ***Challenge: Try tossing the fidget sandwich back and forth between your hands while keeping both layers spinning. This is quite a hard task, so if you can't do it and you're getting frustrated, make yourself a real sandwich (you'll feel better).***

Cap Creativity

Need to rev up the look of your fidget spinner? Pry off or unscrew your spinner's bearing caps. Rub the outside of each cap with sandpaper just a little bit and then wipe with a dry cloth. Now the caps are ready for you to personalize them! Use a permanent marker or some paint to change the color, write your initials, or add a cool saying.

THE TOWER OF POWER

Get together with your friends and stack all of your fidget spinners on top of each other. See how high you can make the tower with all of the spinners still spinning! If you have a big enough group, you can have battles to see which group can build the tallest tower. To ramp up the difficulty, try building your tower on the top of a water bottle (it's harder than it looks!). *Pro Tip: Use sticky tack on the center bearing cap of each layer to build a super strong massive tower. Your friends will think you're a fidget tower wizard!*

Purchasing Ball Bearings

You can buy ball bearings online from major retailers like Amazon and Walmart or fidget spinner specialty stores. You'll also have good luck with companies specializing in skateboard gear. And be sure to check out your local skate or bike shop. Chances are, they're getting lots of visits from spinnerheads and are stocked up on all the right bearings. They'll also be able to give you in-person guidance on installing and cleaning bearings, or they may even do it for you.

THE HIGH-TOSS

To pull off The High-Toss, you'll definitely need to be outside. Hold the fidget spinner between the thumb and index finger of one hand, get it spinning, and then toss it straight up into the air. Try to toss it as high as you can, then catch it between your finger and your thumb. Make sure you keep it spinning for the entire maneuver. Have a competition with your friends to see who can do the highest high-toss. *Pro Tip: Steer clear of areas where there are birds flying overhead. If you hit a bird with your fidget spinner, the entire bird kingdom will track you down and bomb you with bird droppings. Trust me, you don't want that to happen!*

Sleek Style

Wanna take it to the next level? Give your shiny plastic spinner an awesome matte finish. Take off the shine and add the cool! First, remove all of the caps and bearings. Then use fine sandpaper (400 grit works well) and rub the entire spinner to dull the shine. Switch to superfine grit (600 grit) to finish. You can sand the bearing caps, too, or leave them shiny for an eye-catching effect. Wipe everything with a clean cloth and reassemble.

THE HAND FLIP

Start by holding your fidget spinner between the thumb and index finger of one hand with your thumb on top. Get your spinner spinning and then give it a small toss. While the spinner is in the air, flip your hand over and catch the spinner between your thumb and index finger—this time with your index finger on top. *Challenge: Combine the hand flip with The Hot Potato (page 26) or The High-Toss (page 31). See how many times you can do it in a row, and then try to beat your own record!*

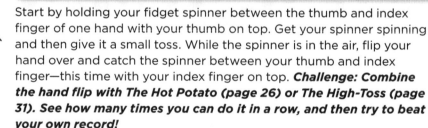

Adventure Edition

If you chose to give your spinner a DIY upgrade with coin weights, try to find some exotic coins to use, like the Danish kroner or the Mexican peso! People will think you're related to Indiana Jones...

DINNER IS SERVED

Dinner is Served is a combination between The Basic Toss (page 25) and The One-Finger Balancing Act (page 24). Start by holding the spinner between the thumb and index finger of one hand. Give it a good spin and then toss it from one hand to the other. When you catch the spinner, instead of snagging it with your thumb and index finger, land it on your index finger without using your thumb at all.
Pro Tip: As tempting as it is, don't do this trick at the dinner table. Your parents will not be happy if you drop your fidget spinner in the mashed potatoes.

Now that you've mastered this trick, you are ready to take the next step into the intermediate section. I'm proud of you. I knew you could do it!

Glow Mojo ←

Ready to see your tricks glow in the dark? Remove all of your spinner's caps and bearings, and put them in a safe spot away from the paint. Place the empty spinner on a paper plate, newspaper, or something else to protect your work surface. Use a paintbrush to completely cover your spinner with glow-in-the-dark paint. You can also paint the outside of the bearing caps. Let everything dry completely, then reassemble.

Jennah Lenae, www.glowartshop.com

THE DOUBLE-DECKER BALANCING ACT

Trick Level - **INTERMEDIATE**

To pull off The Double-Decker Balancing Act, we are going to use a couple of the skills we learned in the beginner section—namely, The One-Finger Balancing Act (page 24) and The Fidget Sandwich (page 29). Start off with a fidget sandwich as the appetizer, making sure both spinners are spinning between the thumb and index finger of one hand with your index finger on the bottom. Then, for the main course, slowly move your thumb away from the top of the spinner. Make sure both spinners stay balanced, spinning on your index finger. *Challenge: If you find this too easy and you're hungry for dessert, step up the difficulty by putting another spinner on top and supersizing your meal to a triple-decker balancing act!*

SPIN GAME: Categories

Make a pointer using a bottle and a fidget spinner. Remove the center bearing cap on one side of the spinner so you have a flat surface. Lay the bottle on its side and tape it to the fidget spinner. Sit in a circle with a group of friends with the pointer in the center. Pick a category like sports teams, superheroes, state capitals—whatever you want! Give the spinner a spin. When it stops, whoever the bottle is pointing toward has to name something in that category. If he names something correctly, continue the game by spinning the spinner again and having the next person name something in the category—no repeats! If the person can't name something, he's out. Keep playing until you are down to one person who is the category champ!

THE 360° TOSSER

You might want to put on your ballet shoes for this trick because your spinner isn't the only thing that will be spinning! For this trick, start out with The High-Toss (page 31). While your spinner is in the air, defying gravity in all its wonderful spinning glory, it's time for the second part of the trick. While your spinner is enjoying some airtime, spin around a full 360°. Once you've completed your spin, catch the spinner between your thumb and index finger and take a bow, because you just completed The 360° Tosser. Nice job. ***Challenge: See if you can spin around twice to turn the 360° tosser into a 720° tosser.***

Pro Tip: When practicing The 360° Tosser, spin the opposite way on each attempt. This way you won't make yourself dizzy by spinning in the same direction all day. Nobody likes getting sick on their fidget spinner because they were reckless with their spin practice—ew.

Stop the Squeak!

If your spinner is making a squeaking or grinding sound, it's time for a cleaning (see page 15). But if you're looking for a quick (temporary!) fix, remove the bearing caps and closures from the top and bottom of the center bearing and spray it with a lubricating spray like WD-40®. Give it a spin to make sure the spray reaches all of the areas in and around the bearing. Continue to apply more spray and spin as needed until your spinner is squeak free!

ROUND THE TWIST

Like many of the other zesty tricks in this book, start as usual by holding the fidget spinner between the thumb and index finger of one hand. Get the fidget spinner spinning, then wrap your arm around behind your back and throw the spinner in the air so it goes between your other arm and your body. At this point, you can snatch the spinner out of the air with either hand, catching it between your thumb and index finger. Then dance around making a monkey sound (the monkey sound is not necessary, I just like doing it myself).
Pro Tip: Do the monkey sound.

Get Your Bearings

Give your fidget spinner a super-cool, industrial look by removing the "armor" (the closure that covers the bearing balls). Be sure to take off all of the closures on all of the bearings, or the weight will be uneven and your spinner won't work well.

UNDER THE LEG, GREG

For this trick all you've got to do is lift up your leg and perform a little alley-oop—toss the spinner under your leg and catch it above your leg. To master this trick, go for a figure eight pattern by tossing the spinner under your right leg from your right hand and catching it in your left hand and then tossing the spinner under your left leg from your left hand and catching it in your right hand. See how many times you can do this in a row, and then try to beat your record! Bonus cool points are awarded if your name is actually Greg.

Cap Swap

If you have a collection of fidget spinners, mix and match the bearing caps from the center bearings to quickly and easily create a custom look. Try covering all of the bearings in one spinner with bearing caps in different colors or patterns.

MD Engineering LLC, www.torqbar.com

THE KNUCKLE DUSTER

This trick seems like a walk in the park, but you'll find it to be one of the hardest tricks in this section to master. The idea is simple: Spin the spinner on your knuckle. But to truly master this trick, there are layers of difficulty that even professional fidgeters have a tough time tackling. *Challenge: Once you have the spinner spinning on your knuckle, try to toss it up in the air and then land it back on your knuckle. This is a very difficult task, so don't be disheartened if you can't get it right away. Hard work is the key to spinner success.*

Splat!

Head outside for this potentially messy paint-splattering project! Take off all of the caps and remove all of the bearings, so you just have the shell of the spinner. Place the spinner on a paper plate or piece of cardboard. Cover the center hole with masking tape (so globs of paint don't get in there and slow down the spinning action). Pour a little paint on another paper plate, a palette, or in a paper cup. Dip your finger, a disposable toothbrush, or a paintbrush in the paint and spritz the spinner. Repeat with additional colors. Let that side of the spinner dry and then flip it over and repeat the process on the other side.

THE HAT TRICK

The hat trick is a special maneuver that ranges in difficulty depending on the style of hat you use. I like to use a flat cap when I bring out The Hat Trick at all the parties I go to, but if you want to step up the difficulty, you can try using a sombrero or one of those cool hats with the propeller on the top. Spinning your fidget spinner on the top of a propeller cap is the perfect way to get some major dual spin action and is a great way to show everyone that you're a real professional fidgeter. *Challenge: Try to walk around in a busy shopping center with the spinner spinning on your hat.*

Wood You?

If you're shopping for a spinner with a really distinctive look, you may be interested in the tons of wood options that are available. Bamboo, walnut, Hawaiian koa—you name a species of wood, and someone has made a spinner out of it. Wood spinners cost a bit more—$20 and up—because they're handcrafted, but that also means each one is totally unique. Etsy is a good place to shop. Or if you're feeling creative, ask the woodworker in your family to help you make your own!

Kyra Tomota, gameprinted.etsy.com

ROUND THE WORLD

For this trick, you will need to start out with The One-Finger Balancing Act (page 24). Once you have the spinner balanced on your finger, you're ready to take the next step. Toss the spinner in the air. Don't toss it too high—eye level is about where you need it. While the spinner is in the air, draw a circle around it with your hand by starting underneath it, bringing your hand around and over the top of it, then back underneath it. To finish this move, land the spinner back on your finger. *Challenge: Try circling your hand around the spinner twice. This is a hard task, so don't worry if you can't get it on the first try. My great grandfather trained for many years developing this trick, and it is only achievable by those with the true essence of the professional fidgeter within them.*

DIY Spinner with Lights

Make your own awesome fidget spinner! You'll need a bearing (a skateboard wheel bearing works well), hot glue, and three LED valve stem lights (the kind you attach to your bicycle tire's valve stem). This way-cool project is simple: just hot glue the metal end of each valve stem light to the outside ring of the center bearing, spacing them evenly around the ring. It lights up when you spin it!

THE TOE TOSS

Remember The Toe Spinner (page 27) back in the beginner section? Well it's back with a vengeance in this pumped-up version. Start by setting up The Toe Spinner. Once you have your spinner rotating on your big toe, it's time to show everybody you mean business. Flick your foot and toss the spinner from the big toe on one foot to the big toe on the other foot. ***Challenge: Try building a small wall between your legs out of building blocks or other household items—your dirty laundry perhaps? The higher the wall you can jump, the more of a master you are. It's just simple math.***

Press Print

By hooking up with a 3D printing service, you can purchase an empty tri spinner housing and add your own bearings and caps for a custom design at a very reasonable price!

Trick Level - **INTERMEDIATE**

Now we're talking. For this trick you'll need two water bottles and a fidget spinner. Try to get water bottles with flat lids, as they will be the easiest to use for this trick. Start by spinning your spinner on the top of one of your water bottles. Then, pick up the water bottle with the spinner in one hand, and pick up the other water bottle with your other hand. Flick the spinner bottle up, tossing the spinner into the air, and land it softly on the top of the other water bottle. Keep tossing the spinner back and forth between the bottles, slowly building your cool points each time you land your spinner successfully.

Rad Hydro-Dip

Your spinner will be completely unique after hydro-dipping it! For this outside project, you'll need a bucket of warm water, 2 or 3 cans of spray paint, a safety mask, and disposable gloves. Remove the caps and bearings from your spinner. With your mask on, spray the colors onto the water in a fun design. Put on those gloves and dip your spinner in the bucket for a few seconds. Remove and let it dry. Put the bearings and caps back on and enjoy your one-of-a-kind spinner!

THE ROCKET

To complete The Rocket, you will need a water bottle with a pop-top lid and you will need to fill it to the very top with water. Pop the lid of your water bottle open, then get your fidget spinner spinning on the top. When you're ready, squeeze the water bottle as hard as you can, shooting water out of the top of the bottle and rocketing your spinner into the air. Now reach up and catch the spinner between your thumb and index finger, ensuring that the spin doesn't stop and the fun times keep on rolling. You will definitely get wet when attempting this move, so consider wearing a raincoat or other protective gear. Also, be sure to dry your spinner quickly and thoroughly after performing this trick (use a hair dryer on the cool setting) or the bearings will rust. You've been warned!

The Batwing

If you're into the world of comics and superheroes, you might be interested in this hugely popular bi-wing spinner variation, which takes its inspiration from the calling symbol of, well, let's just say a certain nighttime vigilante...

SMFX, www.schrockmetalfx.com

THE SKATEBOARD STOMP

Trick Level - *INTERMEDIATE*

For this trick, you will need a skateboard and a fidget spinner. Start by putting the skateboard on the ground, wheels down. Place your spinner on one end of the skateboard and get it spinning. While your spinner is spinning, stomp on the other end of the skateboard, catapulting your spinner into the air. Finish the move by catching the spinner between your thumb and index finger, then ride that skateboard into the distance while the sun sets behind you and never look back. You just completed The Skateboard Stomp. *Pro Tip: Don't stomp the skateboard too hard when practicing. The last thing you want when attempting this trick is to flick the skateboard into your stomach and the spinner into your face and have to spend the rest of the day explaining to everybody how you got that black eye.*

SPIN GAME: The Marathon

Whose fidget spinner can go the longest? Let's find out. You can play this game with a partner or a group. Have everyone place their spinners on a table. At the same time, have everyone give their spinner one spin, then it's hands off! The last spinner spinning wins. Before you challenge anyone to this game, make sure you give your spinner a thorough cleaning (see page 15) for a tip-top performance.

THE SOCCER BALL BALANCER

To attempt this trick, get yourself a soccer ball and a fidget spinner. Make sure the soccer ball is fully inflated, and then balance it on your foot. Once you have the soccer ball balanced on your foot, reach down, place the fidget spinner on the soccer ball, and get it spinning. The aim is to keep the soccer ball balanced on your foot with the fidget spinner balanced on top of the ball and spinning.

Challenge: Try using a football or a pumpkin or anything else you can think of instead of a soccer ball.

Pattern It Up

Customize your spinner with your own pattern. With painter's tape, cover any areas on the spinner where you don't want to change the original color. Using paint, permanent markers, or spray paint (go outside to spray!), color the exposed areas, let it dry, and then carefully remove the tape. You can make stripes or create a camouflage effect so easily!

Jennah Lenae, www.glowartshop.com

THE KNEE KNOCK

The Knee Knock is a classic move in the professional fidgeter's repertoire. You can't consider yourself a pro until you've nailed this trick. To complete this trick, hold your spinner between the thumb and index finger of one hand and get it spinning. Then, making sure to hold your spinner flat, drop it onto your knee and bounce it up off your knee into the air. Once your spinner is getting some airtime, reach out and snatch it between your thumb and index finger, keeping the momentum of the spin. *Challenge: Try bouncing the spinner off both knees before catching it. Also, try bouncing it off your friend's knee. Just make sure your friend knows what you're doing first, because throwing your fidget spinner at your friend's knee without warning is a great way to lose a friend.*

Spintacular Stripes

You can create an epic illusion easily by adding stripes to the prongs of your spinner. Draw the stripes so they go all the way around each prong of your spinner like rings, making sure they line up with each other. You can add as many stripes as you can fit and use different colors. Now, when you spin your spinner, the stripes will blur together in rings of whirling color!

THE GUITAR SUPERHERO

To do The Guitar Superhero, you'll need two extras: a guitar and a cape. If you don't have a cape, you can just use one of your mom's towels (trust me, she won't mind). Wrap the cape around your shoulders and have the guitar in one hand, ready to go. Hold your spinner between the thumb and index finger of your other hand and get it spinning. Now, move it toward the strings on your guitar. Use the spinner to strum the strings of the guitar while you play chords with your other hand. Guitar lessons are required if you want to play anything recognizable, but keep practicing and you'll be the next Jimi Hendrix!

Chameleon Spinner

Wouldn't it be cool if your spinner could change color? It can! Special paints are available at your hardware store or online that will change color when you touch the spinner (called thermochromic paint) or when it gets wet (hydrochromic paint).

THE LAND DOWN UNDER

Trick Level - **INTERMEDIATE**

Start this trick by doing a handstand up against a wall. Once you've nailed that part, get a friend to spin a spinner on the bottom of your foot. To make this move more authentic, you should speak in an Australian accent while doing it. **Challenge: Try doing the handstand without leaning against the wall.**

Pro Tip: If you see someone attempting this trick, help them ramp up the difficulty level by giving them a tickle. Well, maybe don't do that, because that's mean...pretty funny, but mean. It's also a good way to get kicked in the face!

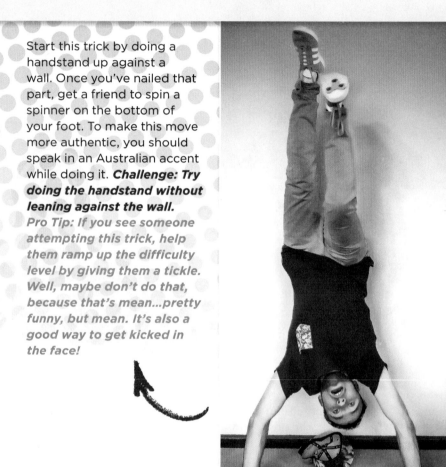

It's the Little Things

If you're just looking for a quick and easy way to jazz up your spinner without a lot of painting and sanding, check online for specialty parts like LED weights and colored bearings. You can usually pick up items like these for a few bucks and pop them into your spinner for a quick and easy upgrade.

PRETTY STICKY

For this trick, you'll need a popsicle or other ice cream treat on a stick and an intense amount of focus. Hold the popsicle straight up, balance the fidget spinner on the tip of the popsicle, and get the spinner going. The aim is to keep the fidget spinner spinning on the tip of the popsicle for as long as possible, even if the popsicle slowly melts and makes your hand and your fidget spinner all sticky. It's certainly not a clean trick and you might need some napkins when you're finished. *Pro Tip: Try this trick with a friend's spinner so you don't get yours all sticky and gross.*

Removable Design

If you don't want to commit to just one look for your spinner, Plasti Dip® may be the way to go. Plasti Dip® spray is a special rubbery, flexible, removable type of paint that you can peel off. First take off the caps and bearings and use painter's tape to cover any spots you don't want to paint. Go outside, put on your safety mask, and spray the Plasti Dip® on your spinner. Let it dry and then reassemble your spinner.

THE MASSIVE DROP

Grab a friend and find an elevated area with a set of stairs or a balcony. Get your friend to stand on the balcony or at the top of the stairs while you stand down in the yard or at the bottom of the stairs. Have your friend get the spinner going and then toss it to you. Try to catch it between the thumb and index finger of one hand.

Challenge: If you've successfully caught the spinner from your friend, try throwing it back and see if your friend can catch it. Bonus cool points will be awarded if you each throw a spinner to each other at the same time and successfully catch them.

There's an App for That!

Fidget spinners have become so popular that companies have already started creating digital versions! A quick search in the app store will yield a multitude of fidget spinner apps. Some of them even allow you to design your own spinner, track your stats, and compete against your friends. While an app may not seem as fun as the real thing, it is silent, so you can use it in places where your actual fidget spinner may not be acceptable.

Wait until the day before you need to put your trash out for collection. The trash can should be very full and very stinky. Get your fidget spinner going and hold it over the bin. While holding your spinner over the bin, do a simple High-Toss (page 31), which you learned in the beginner section of this book. The added stink of the trash along with the possibility that you'll drop your fidget spinner in the stinky trash can and have to fish it out will be the ultimate test of your fidget spinning skill. ***Pro Tip: Try this trick with a friend's spinner so that you don't get yours all stinky and gross.***

Spinning Universe

Want to make your spinner look like a galaxy far, far away? First, remove the caps and bearings, and then sand your spinner to take some of the gloss off so it will hold layers of paint. Set up a spray paint area outside and start with dark blue paint. After letting that layer dry for 5–10 minutes, add a few spots of light blue and magenta. Once those spots are dry, spray some white paint in a plastic cup, dip a toothbrush in it, and flick some "stars" onto your universe. Let it dry and repeat the process on the other side.

THE HARDCORE GAMER

To pull off The Hardcore Gamer, you'll need a video game controller and your favorite video game. Start by placing the fidget spinner on the joystick of your controller. Then, spin the fidget spinner and hold it in place on the joystick with your thumb. Now start playing your video game. Play against your friends, who should all be performing this trick with their fidget spinners, too. *Challenge: Try playing against online opponents who are not performing this trick and see if you can win any games while pulling off The Hardcore Gamer!*

Touch-up Trick

Nail polish is perfect for touching up small scratches on your fidget spinner to make it look like new!

THE COIN FLIP

For this trick, you will need a coin, a water bottle, and a cup. Start by resting the coin on the cap of the water bottle top, leaving a bit of the coin hanging over one edge of the cap. Then, set your cup the other side of the water bottle, opposite the side with the coin hanging over the edge. Hold your spinner between the thumb and index finger of one hand and get it spinning. Then move the spinner toward the overhanging coin until you hit the bottom of the coin, flicking it into the cup. **Challenge: Try standing this book up between the bottle and the cup to act as a wall. Then use your spinner to flick the coin up and over the book wall and into the cup.**
Pro Tip: Smaller coins will fly further, so try different sized coins and see how far you can flick each one.

Now that you've successfully completed the intermediate section, it's time to move on to the advanced section. This is where the tricks start to get really crazy, so stay safe and don't attempt anything you're not ready for!

Paracord Strong

If paracord is tough enough to use in parachutes, it's tough enough for lightning-fast spinning action! Wrap your favorite color around the outside edge of your spinner to measure how much you'll need. Cut the length and ask an adult to singe the ends so it won't fray. Now add a line of glue the whole way around the outside edge of your spinner, and press on that super-strong paracord.

Melissa Pellarin, MeaningfulCreationz.etsy.com

THE DARTBOARD

To pull off The Dartboard, you'll need a dartboard (obviously) and some darts. Start by removing any bearing caps from your fidget spinner. Once you've done this, put a dart through the center bearing in your spinner and pin it to the center of the dartboard. Get your fidget spinner spinning against the dartboard, then throw a dart at it. Try to get your dart through one of the holes at the end of the arms of your spinner. ***Challenge: Try aiming for a specific number on the dartboard, and try to hit that number while also getting your dart through a hole in the fidget spinner.***

Removing Bearings

If you're having trouble removing the bearings from your spinner, use some items around the house to help with the job. Place one of the spinner's circles on top of a roll of clear tape. Now fit the "+" side of a AA battery in the hole of the bearing, and gently tap it with a hammer or a book or even your little sister's Lincoln log. And presto-chango, the bearing pops out!

This one is a tough one to learn, and I certainly do not recommend trying this trick until you have mastered all of the intermediate tricks in this book. It is a combination of The High-Toss (page 31) and The Nose Spinner (page 28). It's simple: begin with a high-toss and then catch the spinner on your nose. This is one of the most difficult tricks in this book and is one that has given me a lot of headaches. It is certainly not for the faint of heart! Don't forget your protective eyewear (sunglasses) for this trick. For extra bonus cool points, try mixing The Massive Drop (page 50) with this trick. But be aware that if you're dropping fidget spinners on your friend's face, you might accidentally ruin your friendship.

Ultra Clean

Toothbrushes or extra tiny dental brushes are perfect for scrubbing your fidget spinner and for getting into all of the nooks and crannies of the ball bearings for a super cleaning.

THE HOUDINI

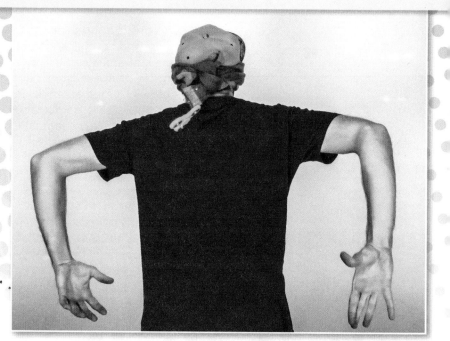

To tackle The Houdini, you must toss your fidget spinner from hand to hand behind your back, with a blindfold on. If you don't have a blindfold, just use a couple of your dad's socks tied together (trust me, he won't mind). It's a difficult task, but if you've made it this far through the trick guide, you should be able to pull it off. **Challenge: Try mixing The Houdini with some of the intermediate tricks in this book by performing them blindfolded.** *Pro Tip: For extra Houdini points, try doing this trick with a straightjacket on.*

Make It 3D

Fidget spinners don't have to be flat. Use hot glue, or super glue, and tweezers to attach beads, rhinestones, or half-marbles to the bearing caps. Let the glue dry, and then check out how insanely awesome your spinner looks when you spin it!

Joshua Murphy, www.FidgetPlanetStore.com

THE JUGGLER

When taking on The Juggler, you will need three fidget spinners. Get all three fidget spinners spinning and then start juggling them the same way that clowns juggle balls. See how many juggles you can do without dropping any of the spinners. You'll probably need to learn how to juggle first... *Pro Tip: The hardest part of this trick is handling three spinning fidget spinners at once. When you're first learning, start your juggle with two spinners and then have a friend toss you the third when you're ready.*

Spinner Art

Make some cool splatter art with your fidget spinner! This technique is messy, so be sure to do it outside with plenty of trash bags and newspaper to protect your clothes and your work surface. Mix some water into acrylic craft paint to make it less thick. Place an old fidget spinner on a piece of paper and pour the watered-down paint onto it. Give the spinner a spin and watch the paint fly over the paper. Give the paint time to dry and repeat with a new color.

THE HIGH-TOSS BACKFLIP

The High-Toss Backflip is just as crazy as it sounds. Start off with The High-Toss (page 31), which you mastered at the start of your journey to fidget glory. Then, I hope you've been brushing up on your gymnastic skills, because it's time for the backflip. Jump straight up into the air, kick your legs back over your head, flip your body around, and land on your feet. If you are not an experienced gymnast, my advice is to start on a trampoline and practice there before you take this trick to the streets. Or substitute the backflip for a less daring move like a cartwheel or forward roll. *Challenge: Try doing The High-Toss Backflip on a motorcycle while jumping over a gigantic fiery pit of scorpions. (I'm joking, please don't try this or your mom will be really angry!)*

Stickers

Stickers are a quick and easy way to customize your fidget spinner! Pop off the bearing caps and trace them on a plain white mailing label sticker. Now you can color the sticker with your own drawing, initials, or message. Cut out the circles from the sticker, apply them to the caps, and reassemble your spinner.

THE DUNNY LIZARD

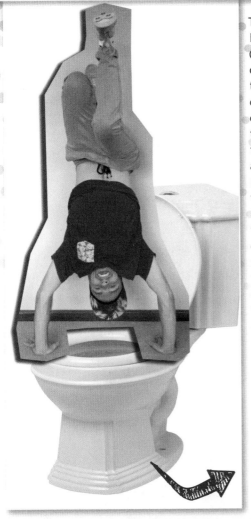

The Dunny Lizard is just like The Land Down Under (page 48), but instead of doing your handstand on the ground, do a handstand over the toilet. The added difficulty of holding onto the toilet seat makes this trick significantly harder and scarier. The Dunny Lizard trick gets its name from the great Australian lizard of the same name that has a strange habit of often hanging around toilets (commonly referred to by Australians as "the dunny"). *Pro Tip: Flush the toilet before you attempt The Dunny Lizard. Trust me. Just do it. Note that the photo used to show this trick is crudely photoshopped. This is due to the fact that this is one trick that I have never tried, nor should you try it. It is a dumb trick that will likely end with your head stuck in the toilet. You've been warned.*

(page 48)

Trick Level - **ADVANCED**

Double Trouble

Increase your spinner's speed by doubling up on the bearings at the end of each arm. Start by pushing the existing bearings halfway out of the fidget spinner's housing so half of the bearing extends beyond the body of the fidget spinner. Now add a second bearing on the other side of the fidget spinner. The extra weight will increase your spinner's momentum and speed!

THE COMBO BREAKER

The Combo Breaker starts off with a few beginner and intermediate moves. The aim is to string together a combination of three beginner moves, then three intermediate moves, and then top it off with a Pocket Drop (itself a separate trick, but one that's best combined with other tricks). To perform a Pocket Drop, all you need to do is throw your spinner up like The High-Toss (page 31) and then catch it in your shirt pocket. If you don't have a pocket on your shirt, just borrow your grandma's sewing machine and sew one onto your shirt. (Trust me, she won't mind. Actually, on second thought, she probably will mind. Definitely ask your grandmother before using her sewing machine.)

Patriotic Spin

If you have a red, white, or blue fidget spinner, you're all set to transform it into a kind of patriotic, spinning flag! Just put painter's tape on the places where you want the color to stay the same, and then use red, white, or blue paint or permanent markers to add the other flag colors. Remove the tape and you're ready to show your American spirit!

THE BIKE TOSS

Trick Level - **ADVANCED** ★ ★ ★

Grab a friend and go out for a ride on your bicycles. Note: Helmets and knee and elbow pads are required for this trick. While you're riding around, start spinning your fidget spinner in one hand. Ride next to your friend and then toss the spinner to your friend to catch. See how many times you can toss the spinner back and forth. To increase the difficulty, ride your bikes further apart from each other. *Pro Tip: Make sure you stay away from busy roads and only ride your bike in areas that are safe and legal to ride in.*

Edible Spinners ◀•••••

Make a mold of your fidget spinner using a silicon mold kit from your local craft store (remove the center bearing before making the mold). Once you have a mold, you can make a fidget spinner out of edible items like ice (water), chocolate, even hard candy. What can you think of to make your own edible fidget spinner?

Nicole Sieff, sweetniks.etsy.com

SLIPPERY SOAP

Cover your fidget spinner in hand soap and then attempt a combination of five intermediate tricks in a row. The hand soap will make your spinner very slippery and very difficult to control. Professional fidgeters are known to use slippery hand soap on their spinners regularly when practicing to really hone their skills. **Challenge: Grab a blindfold and try combining The Houdini (page 56) with Slippery Soap.**

Let It Shine

Get an epic look by using glitter. You'll need Mod Podge, a foam paintbrush, and, of course, some glitter. Remove the bearings and caps and cover the openings in your spinner with painter's tape, so you don't accidentally get any glitter inside the housing that may slow down your spinner. Spread some Mod Podge with the foam brush all over the spinner and then sprinkle glitter over it. Once it's dry, reassemble, give it a spin, and watch it shine!

Jamie Miller, holyghostswag.etsy.com

COVER TO COVER

Take this book, close it, and hold the fidget spinner against the front cover. Start your spinner spinning and then balance it on the front of the book. Flick the book up, tossing your spinner into the air, and then flip the book over, landing the spinner safely on the back cover. ***Challenge: Try tapping the fidget spinner up in the air with the spine of this book as you flip it.*** *Pro Tip: Tell your friends to buy this book; then you can try tossing a spinner from the cover of your book to the cover of a friend's book.*

The Ultra-Lite

If your fidget spinner feels a bit heavy in your hand, you can try removing the weights from the end of each arm. This ultra-light version will be easier for you to manipulate one-handed with your fingers and is also extra quiet.

NOSE TO NOSE

Get together with a friend and start off by doing The Nose Spinner (page 28). Once you have The Nose Spinner perfectly balanced, fling your head up and flick the spinner from your nose, over to your friend's nose. Once your friend lands the spinner perfectly on his or her nose, you've mastered this trick. ***Challenge: Combine this trick with Slippery Soap (page 62). Though if you do this, be aware that you're very likely to get soap in your eye.***

SPIN GAME: Quick Start

Who has the quickest hands? This game can be played with a partner or a group. Take five or more spinners and set them up in a line on a table. The players go one at a time. Have someone act as the timer. When the timer says go, the first person goes down the line of spinners and gets each one spinning. The timer records how long it takes him to start all of the spinners. Stop the spinners and have the next person go. Repeat until everyone has had a chance to spin the line of spinners. Now compare the times to see who was the fastest.

FORTY-TWO

Sit quietly with your spinner in hand and ponder the answer to life, the universe, and everything. *Pro Tip: If this trick does not make much sense to you, get to your local library and check out* The Hitchhiker's Guide to the Galaxy.

Got UV?

Use UV reactive acrylic paint on your fidget spinner to give it a fluorescent glow when it's in black light or strong sunlight. This works best on a white background, so if you have a colored fidget spinner you may want to paint it white first and then add the UV paint. Once the UV paint is dry, you won't see it in normal light, but under black light or intense sunlight the color will pop!

SUPER DOMINO TOWER

To take on this impressive trick, build a huge tower out of dominos. Balance your fidget spinner on the very top of the tower and get it spinning. For extra cool points, cover the tower in hand soap. The higher you build your tower, the harder this trick becomes. Battle your friends and see how high you can build your towers!

Fidget Spinner Fashion

Type "fidget spinner nail art" into YouTube to check out how beauty blogger Natasha Lee created a fully functional mini fidget spinner that she attached to her fingernail. Can you say fidget fashion statement?

ITCHY NOSE TOWER

The Itchy Nose Tower is a combination of The Nose Spinner (page 28) and The Tower of Power (page 30). Get some friends together and stack your spinning spinners on your nose as high as you can. To increase the difficulty, try reciting the alphabet backwards while you stack the spinners. The vibrations on your nose will cause an itching sensation. No matter what, do not give in to the itch! *Pro Tip: Make sure you have a ladder and maybe even a crane ready to go, because you never know how high you'll be able to build an Itchy Nose Tower.*

Warp Speed

Use your phone camera to make your spinner warp! Mount your camera facing a window on a sunny day, and set it at 30 frames per second or lower—the lower the FPS, the better it will look. Now give your spinner a whirl and see how warped it looks on your camera!

HOUDINI JUGGLER FLIP

.For the ultimate, never-been-done trick to end the advanced section, we have the notorious Houdini Juggler Flip. The Houdini Juggler Flip is widely regarded as one of the most difficult fidget spinner tricks ever conceived. Many people have attempted it, but no one has been able to conquer it—yet. To do this trick, start by placing a blindfold over your eyes. When the blindfold is secure, start juggling three spinners, like you learned to do when mastering The Juggler (page 57). When you're ready, toss all three fidget spinners high in the hair, perform a backflip, and finish the move with a Pocket Drop (see The Combo Breaker on page 60), landing all three fidget spinners in your top shirt pocket. Make sure you have a large pocket. *Pro Tip: Hey, if you're attempting this, you're way beyond my skill level. My only tip from here on out is to keep practicing until you're the best fidgeter in the world. That's just the tip you need.*

Soft Grip ◄······

For an extra comfy, soft grip, try gluing mini pompoms to the center bearing caps of your fidget spinner. You can also remove the bearing caps and glue the pompoms directly to the inner ring of the center bearing.

Give a fidget spinner and a copy of this book to every person on earth, generating worldwide happiness and successfully achieving world peace.

Pack 'Em Up

So you need to pick up your spinners from all over the house and put them away? Create a safe storage container with a hardside lunchbox, some foam from the craft store, and scissors. Measure the inside of the lunchbox (length, width, and depth) and cut out a foam piece that will fit inside. Cut slits in the foam for your fidget spinners to sit in. Now you better go pick up those stinky socks...

KNEES AND KNUCKLES

Take forty fidget spinners and spin a tower of ten on the knuckles of each hand and a tower of ten on each of your knees. You must attempt this trick alone with no help from anyone.

Need for Speed

Here's a great way to increase your fidget spinner's speed. Visit your local skate shop and purchase a longboard bearing. They come in a ton of colors and spin super fast. Replace your spinner's center bearing with the longboard bearing and satisfy your need for speed!

THE MEGA TOSS

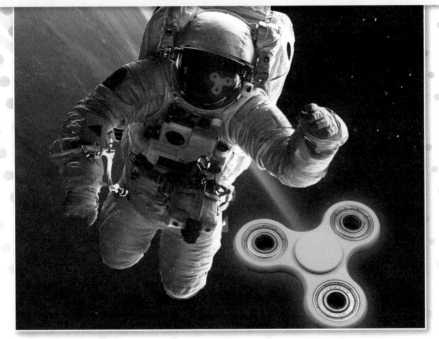

Just like The High-Toss (page 31), throw your spinner high into the sky. While your spinner is in the air, make your bed, do your homework, and watch three videos from your favorite YouTuber (GeekBite, right?). *Pro Tip: The best way to do this trick is to throw your spinner into outer space and get the spinner to orbit around the earth a few times while you do everything you need to do.*

Trick Level - UBER-ADVANCED IMPOSSIBLE BONUS TRICKS !

Get a Grip

Make tricks easier by adding quarters to the center bearing caps of your fidget spinner. If you're willing to donate 50 cents toward trick mastery, this easy hack will create a better grip that will make tossing your fidget spinner from hand to hand and other tricks much easier! Just hot glue a quarter to each center bearing cap (or stick them on with tape doughnuts) and let the games begin!

UNDER THE SEA

Complete tricks 1 through 45 underwater. *Pro Tip: Use scuba equipment.*

Tricking Your Eyes

Transform your spinner into an optical illusion! Draw a circle big enough to completely cover the spinner on construction paper or cardstock, and color it with a mind-bending design. Or search for "optical illusions" online and print a cool design. Cut out the circle. Remove the bearing cap on one side of your spinner so you have a flat surface. Place a small piece of double-sided tape (or make tape doughnuts) on the weights at the end of each arm of your spinner. Press the paper circle in place on top of the spinner. Place your spinner on a hard surface, spin it, and prepare to be amazed!

FAILURE IS NOT AN OPTION

Complete tricks 1 through 45 in a row with only one attempt for each trick. If you fail one of the tricks, you must throw your fidget spinner in the trash and start again.

No Paint? No Problem!

Want that cool, flicked-on painted look for your spinner, but don't have any bottles of paint or spray paint? Nail polish will work just as well! Be warned that it tends to smell a little until it dries. And be warned that moms and sisters may not want their polish used on spinners: your best bet is to ask first!

CHAPTER 4:
Spin Master Workbook

True masters keep track of their accomplishments! Use the Trick Mastery Tracker in this section to track your progress through the tricks in the book. Check off a trick once you've mastered it, and be sure to record the date you nailed it. If you are able to complete any of the Uber-Advanced Impossible Bonus Tricks, we applaud you—you have reached an impossible level of fidget mastery! Use the Trick Stats pages to record the details of all your best tricks. If you want plenty of room to log your improvement, photocopy the stat pages.

TRICK STATS

TRICK NAME	DATE	SPIN TIME	# SPIN

NOTES:

TRICK MASTER TRACKER

Be sure to mark the date you master all your tricks below so you can remember that moment forever!

BEGINNER TRICKS

_____ THE ONE-FINGER BALANCING ACT

_____ THE BASIC TOSS

_____ THE HOT POTATO

_____ THE TOE SPINNER

_____ THE NOSE SPINNER

_____ THE FIDGET SANDWICH

_____ THE TOWER OF POWER

_____ THE HIGH-TOSS

_____ THE HAND FLIP

_____ DINNER IS SERVED

INTERMEDIATE TRICKS

_____ THE DOUBLE-DECKER BALANCING ACT

_____ THE 360° TOSSER

_____ ROUND THE TWIST

_____ UNDER THE LEG, GREG

_____ THE KNUCKLE DUSTER

_____ THE HAT TRICK

_____ ROUND THE WORLD

_____ THE TOE TOSS

_____ THE WATER BOTTLE TOSS

_____ THE ROCKET

_____ THE SKATEBOARD STOMP

_____ THE SOCCER BALL BALANCER

_____ THE KNEE KNOCK

_____ THE GUITAR SUPERHERO

_____ THE LAND DOWN UNDER

_____ PRETTY STICKY

TRICK MASTERY TRACKER

Be sure to mark the date you master all your tricks below so you can remember that moment forever!

_____ THE MASSIVE DROP

_____ TAKING OUT THE TRASH

_____ THE HARDCORE GAMER

_____ THE COIN FLIP

ADVANCED TRICKS

_____ THE DARTBOARD

_____ HEADS UP

_____ THE HOUDINI

_____ THE JUGGLER

_____ THE HIGH-TOSS BACKFLIP

_____ THE DUNNY LIZARD

_____ THE COMBO BREAKER

_____ THE BIKE TOSS

_____ SLIPPERY SOAP

_____ COVER TO COVER

_____ NOSE TO NOSE

_____ FORTY-TWO

_____ SUPER DOMINO TOWER

_____ ITCHY NOSE TOWER

_____ HOUDINI JUGGLER FLIP

UBER-ADVANCED IMPOSSIBLE BONUS TRICKS

_____ CAN'T WE ALL JUST GET ALONG?

_____ KNEES AND KNUCKLES

_____ THE MEGA TOSS

_____ UNDER THE SEA

_____ FAILURE IS NOT AN OPTION

TRICK NAME	DATE	SPIN TIME	# OF SPINNERS

NOTES:

_____

_____

_____

_____

_____

TRICK NAME	DATE	SPIN TIME	# OF SPINNERS

NOTES:

_____

_____

_____

_____

_____

TRICK NAME	DATE	SPIN TIME	# OF SPINNERS

NOTES:

_____

_____

_____

_____

_____